OPERANTICS

WITH
WOLFGANG AMADEUS MOZART

TEXT BY
Mary Neidorf

ILLUSTRATIONS BY
Daniel Stevens

GAMES BY
Jan Fruman
AND
Daniel Stevens

Color this page in your favorite colors

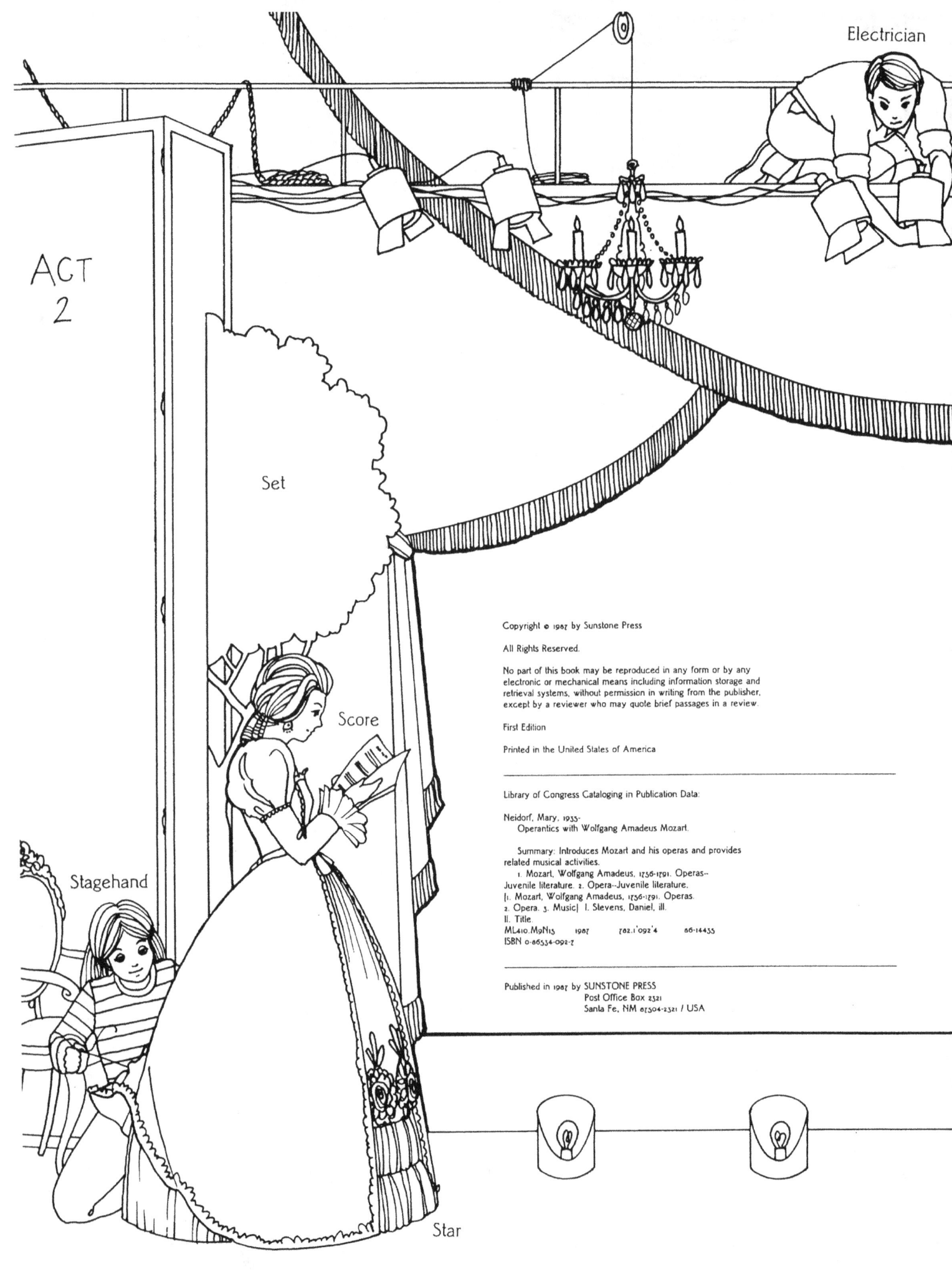

CONTENTS

What is an Opera? / 4

About Opera Singers / 4-5

Mozart / 6-9

Grand Tour Maze / 10-11

"Watch" Game / 12

Play Mozart's "Minuet in G" / 13

Instruments in an Orchestra / 14-15

The Marriage of Figaro / 16-17

Don Giovanni / 18

Cosi Fan Tutte / 19

The Magic Flute / 20-21

Puppets for "The Magic Flute" / 22-23

Hidden Picture / 24-25

Musicrossword / 26

Answers / 27

Color this picture in your favorite colors

WHAT IS AN OPERA?

An opera is a play whose words are sung. The singers are highly trained singing actors who are familiar with both music and with the theater, for opera is a combination of both. The music is written to be played by an orchestra. As in any play, the acting is supervised by the Director. But because everything depends on the music in the first place, the Conductor is the most important supervisor in the opera theater. The musicians call the Conductor "Maestro" (pronounced My-stro), an Italian word meaning "master."

Why are there so many Italian words used in the opera theater? Words like "aria," meaning "song"; "bravo," a word the audience shouts which means "hurrah." The word "opera" is itself an Italian word which means "work." Why are so many of these terms Italian? It is because opera began in Italy.

About 400 years ago a group of musicians and poets in Florence, Italy, met together. They wanted their songs to express feelings and tell stories as had the old Greek dramas (plays) of long ago. Their group was called the "Camerata," another Italian word. It means "room," for they first met in rooms in the houses of two noblemen.

The first opera, DAFNE, was written by Jacopo Peri in 1597. In 1600, Peri's opera EURIDICE (pronounced You-ri-di-chey) was the first opera ever to be performed in public. A new art form had been created, one which combined stories, dance, music and theater; one which we still enjoy.

ABOUT OPERA SINGERS:

Without singers, there could be no opera. Here is a little guide to the different voices.

SOPRANO — the highest woman's voice, usually ranging two octaves above middle C on the piano. In opera stories, the soprano is often the young heroine.

MEZZO-SOPRANO — the next highest woman's voice. Young boy roles are often written for this voice and played by women. These roles are called "trouser" roles.

CONTRALTO or ALTO — the lowest woman's voice. She is often the old woman, the unloved younger woman or the servant.

TENOR — the highest man's voice, usually ranging from an octave below middle C to an octave above. The tenor is usually the young lover or hero.

BARITONE — the next lowest man's voice. In opera, he is often the jealous husband or the hero's best friend. Sometimes he is the comic hero.

BASS — the lowest man's voice. This voice, very deep, often sings the role of the king or of a very old man.

ABOUT MOZART:

Mozart was one of the greatest composers of opera and his compositions are performed constantly all over the world. You'll enjoy reading about him on the following pages.

MOZART

In the beautiful town of Salzburg in western Austria, set in the midst of the Bavarian Alps of Europe and surrounded by green forests and the river Salzach, Mozart was born. No one, looking at the tiny blue-eyed baby, could have guessed that during his 35 years, he would write hundreds of musical compositions and bring fame to his family and even to the town of Salzburg, itself.

"What shall we call him?", asked his older sister, Marianne. She was four-and-a-half years old, and very excited to have a new brother. "Wolfgang," her father replied. (In Austria, where the German language is spoken, all "W's" sound like "V's".) "I shall call him 'Wolferl'," she declared, for she herself had a nickname: it was "Nannerl." The next day the baby was taken to the cathedral and christened "Joannes Chrysostomus Wolfgang Gottlieb Mozart." "Gottleib" means "beloved of God"; later, Mozart began to use the Latin form of the same name, "Amadeus" (pronounced Ahm-ah-day-us). And so we know him today as Wolfgang Amadeus Mozart, one of the world's greatest composers.

Salzburg

How do little babies grow up to be great, famous men and women? No one really knows the answer to that question. But this is the story of one such baby.

The Mozarts lived on the third floor of an old Salzburg house. His mother, Anna Marie, had no musical talent but was a happy wife and loving mother. However, Mozart's father, Leopold, was a violist-composer employed by the prince-bishop whose castle sat high on the hill above the town. It was Leopold's job to play in the Archbishop's private orchestra and to compose special music for church services in the cathedral. Since his salary was not a large one, he taught pupils privately at his home. And musician friends often came to the house to play string trios and quartets. Nannerl was a talented little girl so her father gave her lessons on the clavier. The clavier was a small stringed instrument much like a piano. So young Mozart was surrounded with music from the day he was born. His first steps took him to the clavier.

When Mozart was three he would stand at the keyboard making pleasant sounds; he never pounded as some small children do. He begged his father to give him lessons. Father Mozart would put the tiny hands on the keys and show his young son how to sound the notes. At the age of four, Wolfgang was playing minuets; at five, he was composing pieces of his own. Nannerl and Wolfgang, both so talented and so young, became known in Salzburg as the "Wonder Children."

Color Mozart's portrait

When he was almost six, Mozart was given a child-size violin by one of his father's friends. Leopold refused to give him violin lessons, saying that piano lessons and other musical studies in harmony were enough for so young a child. But, all alone, Wolfgang learned to play the new instrument. One day his father's friend, Herr Schachtner, and Herr Wenzel, another musician, came to the Mozart home to play some new trios for strings. Wolfgang begged to be allowed to play second violin along with Herr Schachtner. Telling him to play very quietly so the sour notes would not be heard, permission was given. Soon, Herr Schachtner stopped playing altogether; all were amazed that the child played the part without a mistake. After that, violin lessons were added to his musical studies.

The Mozart house was a busy, happy place. Besides the family there was a canary, (Herr Canari sang in the key of G major when he was happy, Wolfgang said), a kitten and a dear little dog named Bimberl. But there was never enough money. Papa Mozart began to think of taking his "wonder children" on a concert tour, to display them to all of Europe and to make more money. So it was that the children, accompanied by their father, set out in a horse-drawn coach with their luggage and the little clavier tied on top heading for Munich over 100 miles away, to play before the Prince of Bavaria. Nannerl was almost eleven years old and Wolfgang not yet six. The trip lasted three weeks and the children were received kindly. Next came a journey to Vienna, the capital of Austria, where Leopold hoped to find wealth and fame. This time Mamma Mozart came along. The children were invited to the Royal Palace to play before Empress Maria Theresa. Wolfgang and Nannerl played duets on the piano and Wolfgang also played alone. Then he played the violin, accompanied by his sister. They went to the Palace every day to perform for guests. Afterwards they played games with children of the royal family. The Empress gave to each of the children an outfit of silk and gold braid, and to Leopold 100 gold pieces. With Wolfgang's suit came a small but splendid sword.

Six months later, the family was again traveling. While the children traveled they continued to study from workbooks Papa had prepared for them. They learned languages, reading and arithmetic. On this

Grand Tour they played before kings and queens and gave public concerts in Frankfurt, Germany; Brussels, Belgium; Paris, France; London, England; and The Hague, Holland. Finally, after three years of travel, they came home to Salzburg.

The trip had not been the financial success that Papa Mozart had hoped for. Yet the children, and especially Wolfgang, were now famous. Other things of lasting effect had happened to the young genius, also. In Paris, he saw an opera for the first time and loved it. In London, he again saw operas performed, but this time they were Italian operas, not so serious as the French. They had joy and humor. It was in London, too, that Mozart wrote his first symphony. He was only eight years old.

After the Grand Tour, Wolfgang's musical education and concert career continued. Nannerl did not accompany him for she was growing up and at fifteen was no longer a "Wonder Child." Mozart continued to compose. The PRETENDED SIMPLETON, his first opera, was written when he was twelve, but the musicians refused to perform it because they were sure that anything written by one so young could not be any good. However, his opera BASTIEN AND BASTIENNE, was performed that same year.

More tours, some short, some longer like the one to Italy, came and went. His opera MITHRIDATES, KING OF PONTUS was produced in Milan with fifteen-year-old Mozart conducting. Surely great fortune would follow fame? But wealth would never be possible for Mozart. Another kind of wealth, the wealth of genius, was his only fortune.

While Mozart was appreciated as a composer, teacher, piano performer, no permanent position was offered. And often instead of money he received gifts. In a letter to his father he complained "I have five watches. I have a good mind to have an extra pocket made and wear two watches so that people will see that I do not need another."

After leaving Paris, where his mother died, Mozart gave up playing the violin and devoted his time to the piano and composing. At this time, he was in love with a young girl named Aloysia Weber, but eventually he married her younger sister, Constanze. Constanze was neither wealthy nor of an important family which did not please Mozart's father, but Wolfgang and Constanze were happy together. She would sing or read to him while he composed in the evening. They had two sons, but neither one showed any special interest or ability in music. Constanze and Wolfgang lived in Vienna where Wolfgang taught pupils privately and continued to give concerts. He became known as the finest pianist in Europe.

Mozart's last years were filled with triumphs and disappointments. In 1787, when he was thirty-one years old, he was appointed Concert Master in the Court of the Emperor Joseph in Vienna. Mozart enjoyed a close friendship with the famous composer Haydn. He composed his finest operas during this time, operas which carried his fame throughout Europe: COSI FAN TUTTE, DON GIOVANNI, THE MARRIAGE OF FIGARO and THE MAGIC FLUTE.

But along with fame came debts and illness. Finally, in the winter before he was thirty-six years old, Mozart died. Since Constanze was too ill to go to the cemetery no one ever knew exactly where Mozart was buried. In 1859, the city of Vienna raised a monument in St. Stephens Cemetery on the spot where it is thought the grave might be.

But his true monument is in the hundreds of beautiful compositions which he left for people of all ages and countries to enjoy.

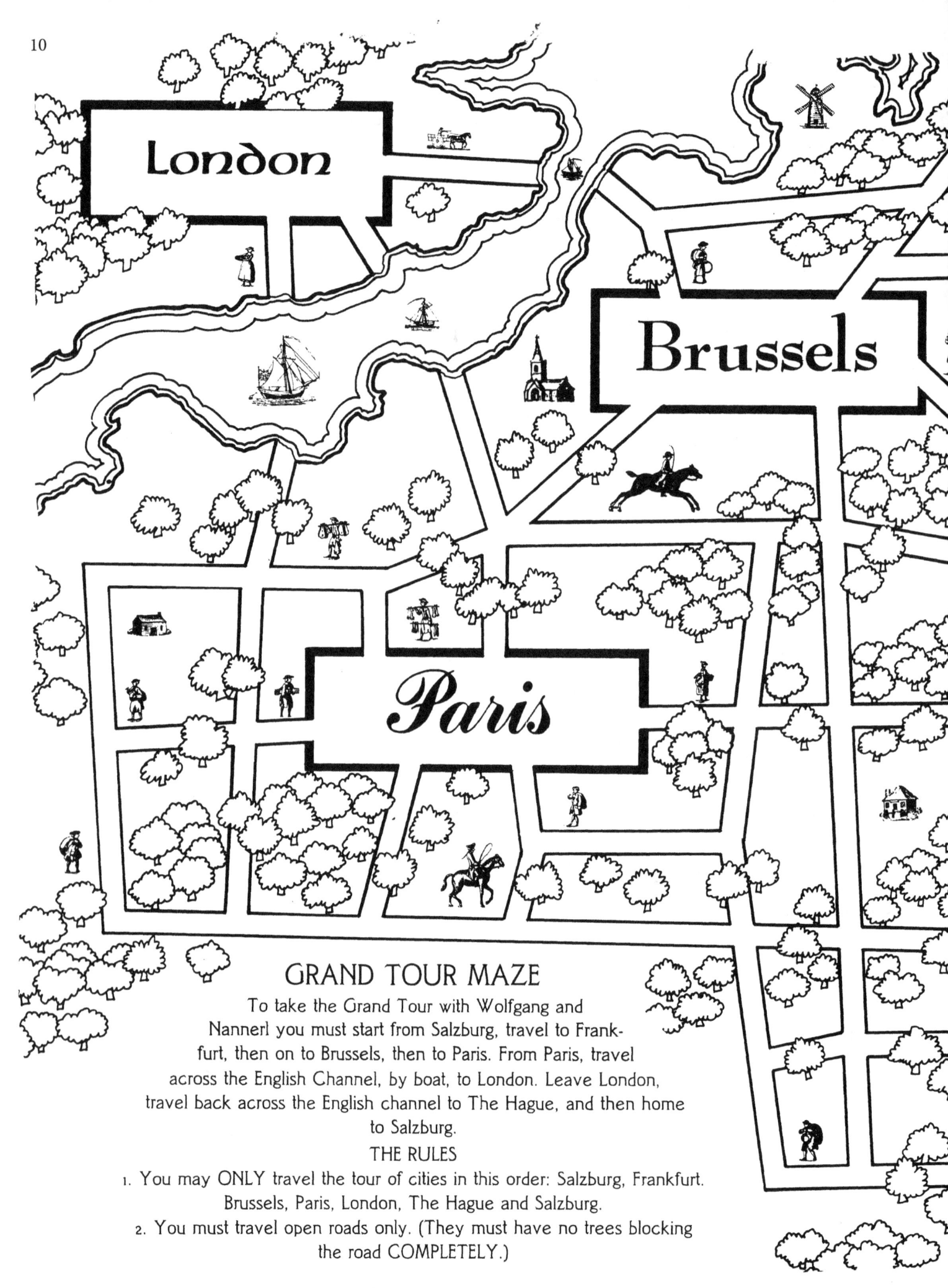

GRAND TOUR MAZE

To take the Grand Tour with Wolfgang and Nannerl you must start from Salzburg, travel to Frankfurt, then on to Brussels, then to Paris. From Paris, travel across the English Channel, by boat, to London. Leave London, travel back across the English channel to The Hague, and then home to Salzburg.

THE RULES

1. You may ONLY travel the tour of cities in this order: Salzburg, Frankfurt, Brussels, Paris, London, The Hague and Salzburg.
2. You must travel open roads only. (They must have no trees blocking the road COMPLETELY.)

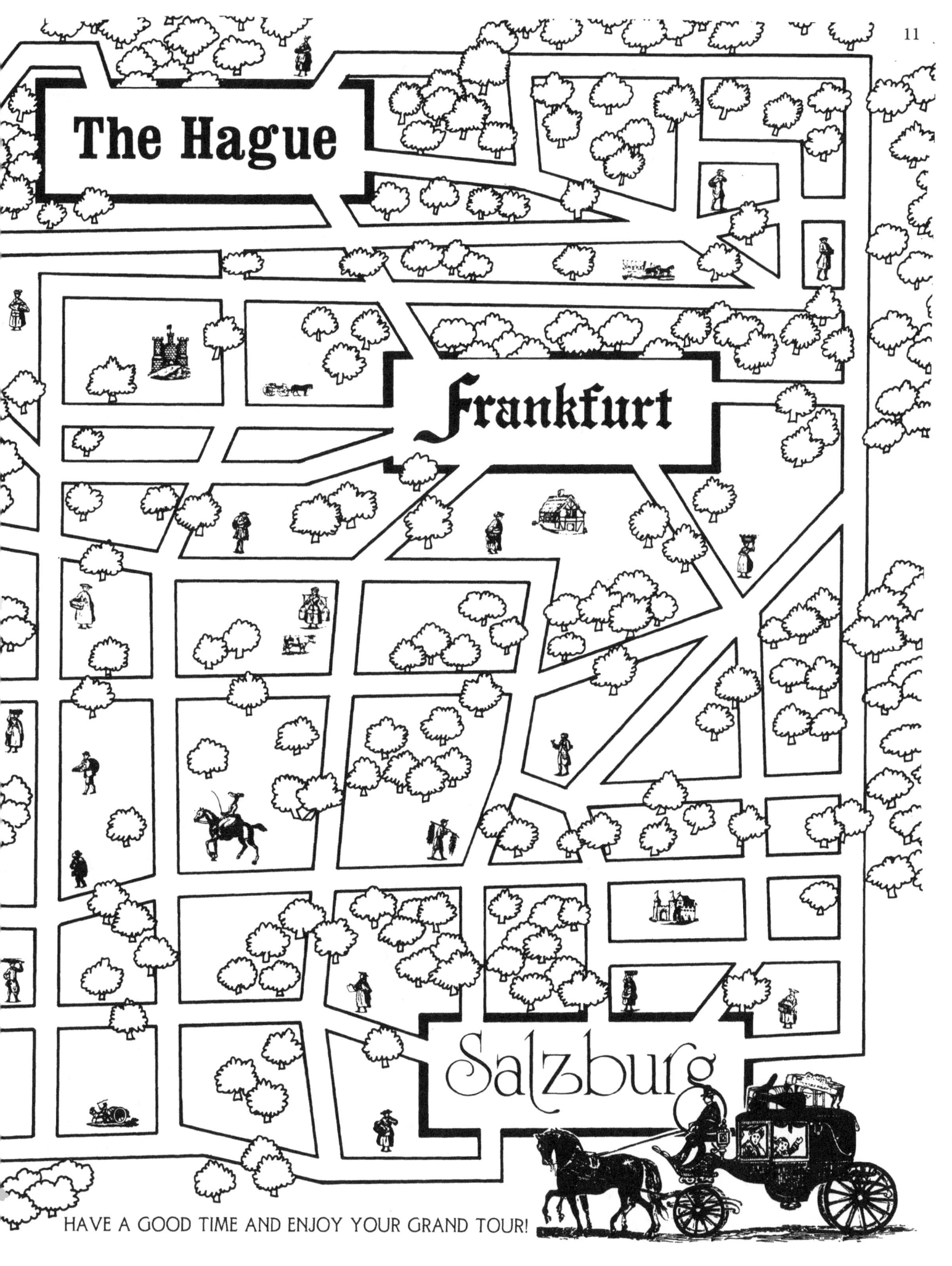

Mozart was given too many watches and not enough money!

If you ever receive more pocket watches than you have pockets, you might play this game with them.

DIRECTIONS FOR PLAYING

Cut out all of the watches on the left hand side of the page, or, if you don't want to do that much cutting, get 14 buttons, or beans, or pennies, instead; and lay them over the 14 watches in the picture. The players take turns picking up the watches. Each player can pick up either one, two or three watches at each turn. (The player may decide differently each time.) The player who picks up the last watch loses. There is a trick to this game. Maybe you will catch on to it after you've played it a few times.

PLAY MOZART'S "MINUET IN G"
(Composed in 1761, when he was 5 years old!)

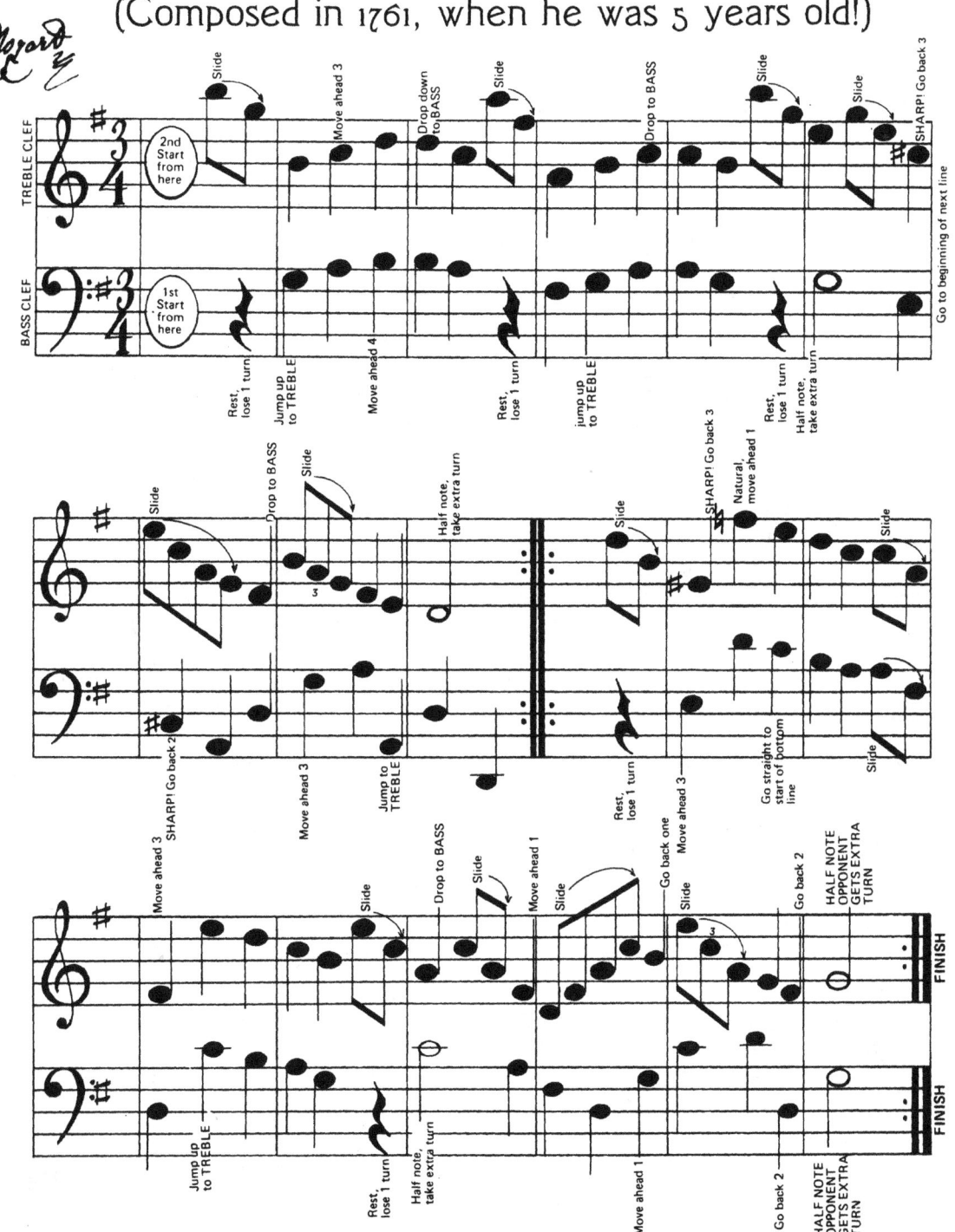

(If you have enjoyed the 1st half of Mozart's Minuet in G on the piano, the entire minuet may be found at the music store.)

INSTRUCTIONS:
1. Each player chooses a different small object to be his marker.
2. Players toss a coin to see who goes first.
   How to toss a coin: a) Have your opponent call out loud either "heads" or "tails." b) Throw your coin in the air (not too high). c) If coin lands with the same side up that opponent called, then he or she goes first. d) If coin lands with the different side up than opponent called, then you go first.
3. Player who goes first begins on BASS CLEF (bottom lines), just past the 𝄢
4. Player who goes second begins his turn on TREBLE CLEF (top lines), just past the 𝄞
5. Take turns tossing coin and move left to right:

Heads = move ahead 1 note. Tails = move ahead 2 notes.
6. Follow any instructions written beside a note you land on. Rests (𝄽) count as a note.
7. If opponent lands on a note you are already on, move ahead 1 note and follow any instructions written on it before your next turn.
8. If you are told to drop down to BASS CLEF or jump up to TREBLE CLEF, move to the note directly below or above the note you are on. Then move ahead staying in in the new clef.
9. After the last note, must toss "head" to win.
   First person to read finish finishes playing the MINUET in G and wins the music award.

Color the Instruments

14

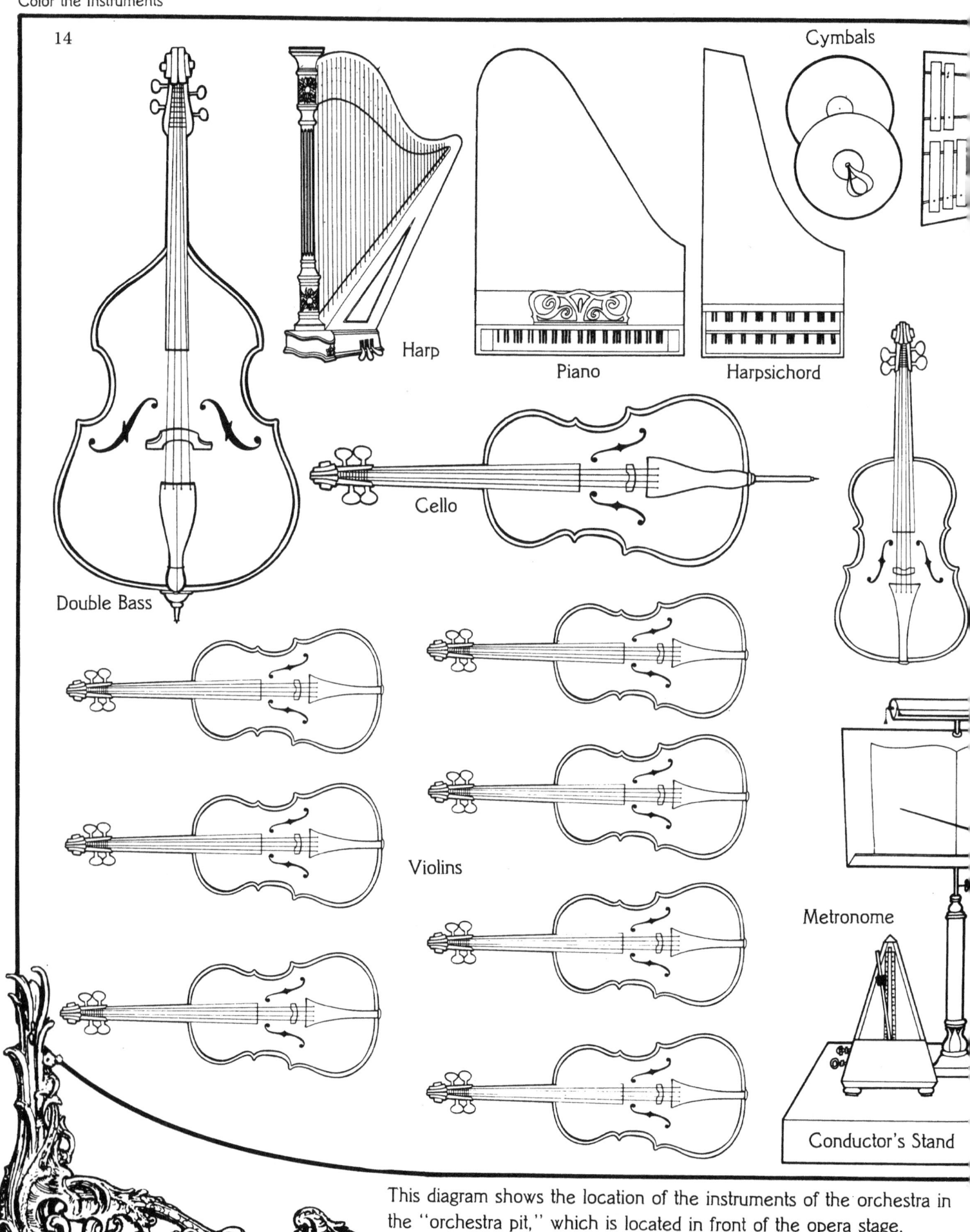

Cymbals
Harp
Piano
Harpsichord
Double Bass
Cello
Violins
Metronome
Conductor's Stand

This diagram shows the location of the instruments of the orchestra in the "orchestra pit," which is located in front of the opera stage, below stage level.

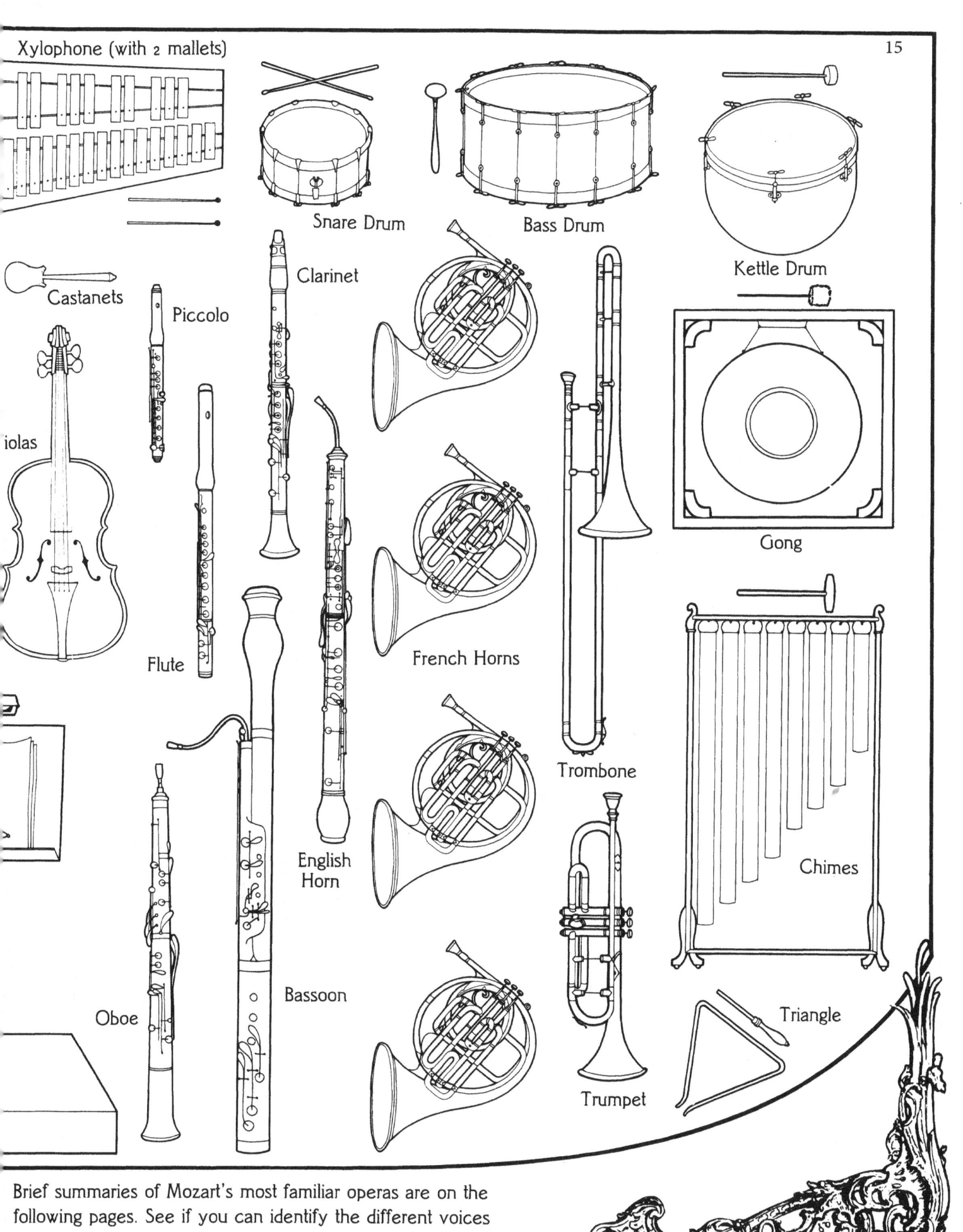

Brief summaries of Mozart's most familiar operas are on the following pages. See if you can identify the different voices for the parts.

THE MARRIAGE OF FIGARO

It is the wedding day of Figaro and Susanna. Figaro is angry at the Count for flirting with Susanna and for delaying the wedding. As the Count continues pursuing Susanna, the Countess is sure her husband no longer loves her, and joins in a plot. She decides to make the Count jealous by pretending that she is in love with someone else. The Count becomes certain that his rival is the young Page, Cherubino, and sends him away to the army. But the boy sneaks back to say goodbye to the Countess. Suddenly the Count knocks on the door and Cherubino has to leap over a balcony into the flower garden to escape. Just as all seems well, Antonio the gardener arrives with a broken flower pot, and tells the Count that a man was thrown off the balcony. Things become very mixed up and Figaro barely escapes marrying the old Marcellina. Finally, after much confusion, Marcellina marries Dr. Bartolo, Figaro marries Susanna and the Count and Countess are reunited.

DON GIOVANNI

The opera tells the story of a handsome, wealthy man, Don Giovanni who seeks his own pleasure no matter who he harms, and of his awful fate. As the opera begins, he attacks a young girl and kills her father in a sword fight. Don Giovanni and Leporello, his servant, again battle to avoid being punished for the murder and escape through a window as his masked enemies try to capture him. Finally, the statue of the murdered father appears and demands that Giovanni ask God's forgiveness for his evil life. When the Don refuses, fire engulfs the mansion and Don Giovanni vanishes in the flames.

COSI FAN TUTTE

Ferrando and Guglielmo are in love with Fiordiligi (Fee-or-dee-lee-gee) and Dorabella who are sisters. The men agree to Don Alfonso's plot to test the girls' love for them. Pretending to march off to war, the youn men return in disguise and try to win the sisters' love. In one funny scene in the opera, the young masqueraders rush in with bottles of poison which they pretend to drink. Despina, who is in on the game, disguises herself as a doctor and restores them to health with the aid of tubes and other equipment which she says are the latest medical discoveries. The girls give in to the pretend-lovers and Don Alfonso wins his bet. But the opera ends happily with the lovers vowing to love one another forever.

THE MAGIC FLUTE

Prince Tamino faints with fear of a giant Dragon-like serpent. Suddenly three magical warrior maids appear and kill the monster. Then the Queen of the Night appears and asks Tamino to save her beautiful daughter, Pamina, from the evil Sarastro. Tamino falls in love with Pamina's picture. Papageno, the Queen's bird-catcher, is ordered to go along on the search. Tamino is given a magic flute whose music will protect him wherever he goes, and Papageno receives magic bells.

Papageno obeys, for he is afraid of the Queen, although what he would really like to find is a little wife for himself. Wandering away from Tamino, Papageno finds Pamina but also learns that Sarastro's temple is not evil but founded on the highest ideals of Truth and Goodness; it is the Queen who is the evil one. Prince Tamino and Papageno are led away, for to be worthy of Love and Brotherhood they must pass tests requiring great courage. Papageno fails the tests but, encouraged by three kindly Spirits, he plays the magic bells. Suddenly, a lovely little Papagena appears. Tamino and Pamina pass together through the dangerous caves of fire and water protected by the music of the magic flute Tamino plays. As the lovers are united before the Temple of the Sun, the evil Queen of the Night and her guards sink from sight.

On the next page are puppets you can use for your own opera production.

Here is a pattern for you to use to make puppets for your own production of "The Magic Flute." Draw in and color the face and clothing.

WARNING: Don't cut out finger puppets until you have finished the Hidden Picture and THE MAGIC FLUTE coloring page.

Color in the faces and clothing. Then cut out finger puppet along heavy dark line. Fold tab back along dotted line and paste tab to the back of the other side to form a cone shape.

23

HIDDEN PICTURE

The stage is set; the opera is about to begin.
But wait! — some of the members of the orchestra cannot find their instruments. Look closely at the picture and see if you can find them. The missing instruments are: Snare Drum, Piccolo, English horn, Harp, Castanets, Triangle, Xylophone, French horn. And, oh yes! — the Metronome is there, too. If you don't know what these instruments look like turn back to pages 12 and 13.

After you have found the lost instruments, color the picture

_____ Set	_____ Director
_____ Backstage	_____ Tragedy
_____ Star	_____ Script
_____ Stagehand	_____ Stage
_____ Electrician	_____ Comedy

1. Place in the theater where play is performed.
2. A person in a principal acting part or "role."
3. Person who tells actors what to do and how to do it.
4. Book with all the actors' words or "lines" in it.
5. Part of the stage unseen by the audience.
6. Person who moves scenery and gets the stage ready.
7. Person who operates the stage lighting.
8. Scenery and furniture for the play or opera.
9. A funny, happy play.
10. A sad, serious play.

Here are some words you will hear if you go to the theater or act in a play. Since opera is also a type of theatrical performance these terms are used by singers and everyone who watches operas or works with them. Find the correct definition for each word and write its number in the blank.

MUSICROSSWORD

ACROSS

3 Mozart's last opera (2 words)
6 The notes of the scale are do, re, mi, fa, so, ___, ti, do
7 Opposite of before
9 _____ FAN TUTTE
11 A play set to music
12 Many musical _____s make an orchestra
16 The first note of the scale
17 When you finish the puzzle, turn this _____
18 The orchestra's leader
20 Not yes
21 _____ Giovanni
22 Two people singing or playing music
24 A big church organ has this; also men smoke them
25 Beautiful string instrument that angels play
26 Not go
29 Woman's middle singing voice: _____-soprano
30 A song in opera (it means "air" in Italian)

DOWN

1 Woman's lowest singing voice: CONTR+_____
2 Applaud; hit your hands together
4 A division of an opera; or to perform on stage
5 Man's middle singing voice
6 Mozart visited England's capital city
8 COSI _____ TUTTE
9 Someone who writes music
10 You sing this
13 A brass instrument (often used for signaling like a bugle)
14 You listen to music with this
15 Man's highest singing voice
19 ♪ is one
22 Percussion instrument that you beat
23 Not down
26 The fifth note of the scale
27 Leopold was Wolfgang's _____
28 The third note of the scale

ANSWERS

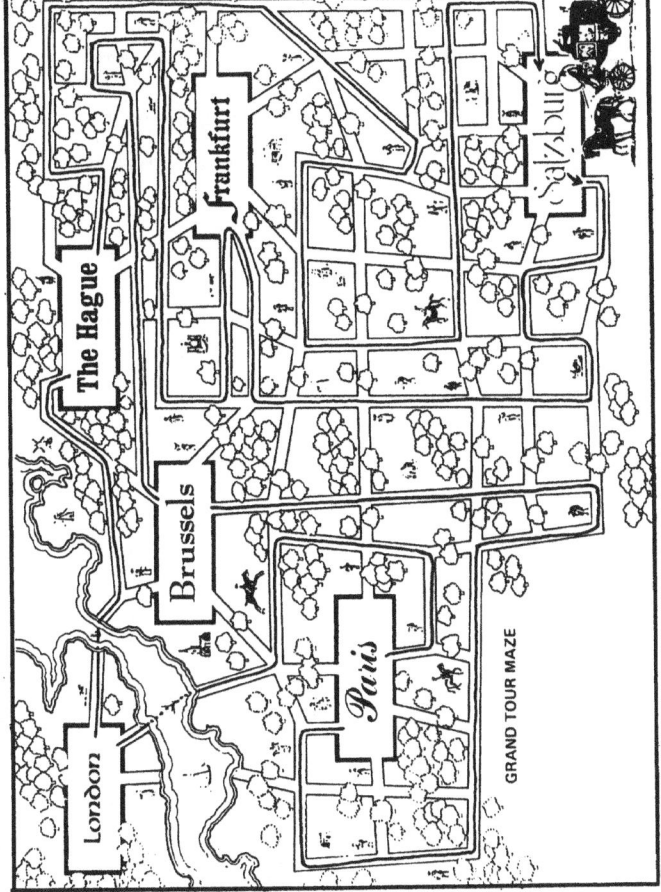

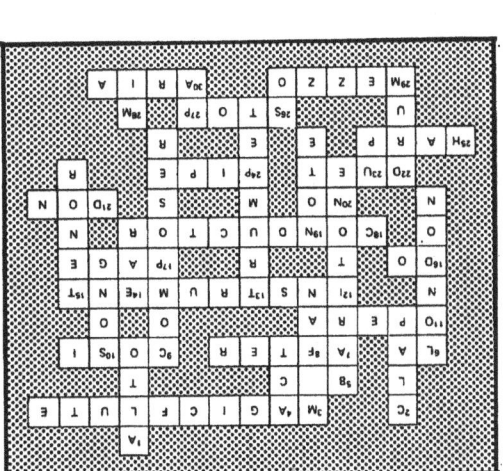

Hidden Picture Answers: Triangle at top of right hand column; Snare Drum at bottom of right hand column; Piccolo in center of chandelier; English Horn in center of flower urn; Harp in center of stair steps; Xylophone at center of banister; Castanets on drapery tassel; Metronome upside down on flower urn pedestal; French Horn in top section of drape.

* * * * *

Theater Quiz Answers: 1. Stage; 2. Star; 3. Director; 4. Script; 5. Backstage; 6. Stagehand; 7. Electrician; 8. Set; 9. Comedy; 10. Tragedy.

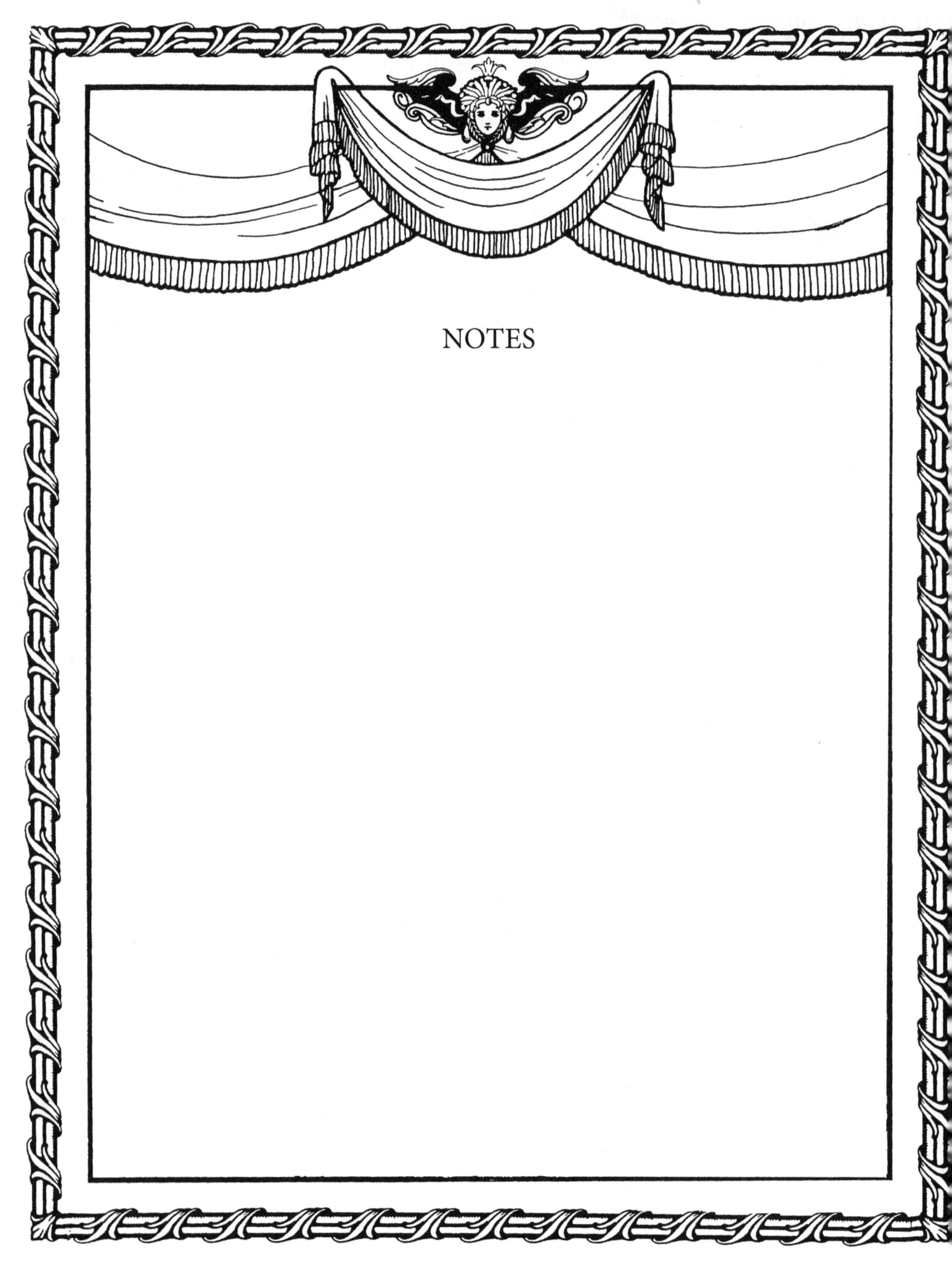

NOTES

www.ingramcontent.com/pod-product-compliance
Lightning Source LLC
Chambersburg PA
CBHW081509040426
42446CB00017B/3448